AUDIE MURPHY
WAR HERO AND MOVIE STAR

AUDIE MURPHY
WAR HERO AND MOVIE STAR

Judy Alter

Illustrated by Patrick Messersmith

State House
Press

McMurry University
Abilene, Texas

Library of Congress Cataloging-in-Publication Data

Alter, Judy, 1938-
    Audie Murphy : war hero and movie star / Judy Alter ; illustrated by
    Patrick Messersmith.
        p. cm.—(Stars of Texas series)
    Includes bibliographical references and index.
    ISBN-13: 978-1-933337-19-7 (hbk.: alk. paper)
    ISBN-10: 1-933337-19-2 (hbk.: alk. paper) 1. Murphy, Audie, 1924-1971
2. United States. Army—Biography—Juvenile literature. 3. World War, 1939-1945—
Campaigns—Western Front—Juvenile literature. 4. Medal of honor—Biography—
Juvenile literature. 5. Soldiers—United States--Biography—Juvenile literature.
6. Motion picture actors and actresses—United States—Biography—Juvenile literature.
I. Title.

U53.M87A58 2007
940.54'21092--dc22
[B]

2007034006

State House Press
McMurry Station, Box 637
Abilene, TX 79697-0637
(325) 572-3974
www.mcwhiney.org/press

Distributed by Texas A&M University Press Consortium
(800) 826-8911
www.tamu.edu/upress

Printed in the United States of America

ISBN-13: 978-1-933337-19-7
ISBN-1-933337-19-2

Book designed by Rosenbohm Graphic Design

THE STARS OF TEXAS SERIES

Other books in this series include:
Henrietta King: Rancher and Philanthropist
Mirabeau B. Lamar: Second President of Texas
Miriam "Ma" Ferguson: First Woman Governor of Texas
Martín de León: Tejano Empresario

Free workbooks available on-line at
www.mcwhiney.org/press

CONTENTS

INTRODUCTION

✳✳✳✳✳

Audie Murphy was the most decorated soldier during World War II. He was awarded the Medal of Honor, the highest military award for bravery given to any individual who risks his or her life above and beyond the call of duty.

Audie Murphy's life was shaped by three things: the Great Depression of the 1930s, World War II of the 1940s, and a Hollywood career which began in the early 1950s and continued through the 1960s. The Depression and his family's poverty toughened him. The war was the experience that followed him all his life and brought him fame. Hollywood was never like real life to him. Of the three, war was the definitive experience of his life.

Murphy was a young boy during the Great Depression. This was a period of severe economic hardship that began with a stock market crash in October 1929 and lasted through the 1930s and into the 1940s.

Murphy was born on a small farm in Northeast Texas in 1924. His father did not own the land and was a share-cropper. The family was very poor, and by the time Audie was a teenager, Depression and drought had settled over the region. Poverty and gritty sand were everywhere. Audie Murphy joined the army in June 1942, just days after his eighteenth birthday. He wanted to get away from his life in Texas and to serve his country.

In addition to the Medal of Honor, he was awarded the Distinguished Service Cross, the Silver Star with Oak Leaf Cluster, the Bronze Star Medal, the Purple Heart with Oak Leaf Cluster, a Good Conduct Medal, a World War II Victory Medal, and others in his three years of active military service. France and Belgium awarded him five medals. He was clearly the most

During the Great Depression, banks failed and many people lost their jobs and their homes. Some people could not feed their families and they stood in "bread lines" waiting for free food.

famous hero of World War II. His accomplishments during his three years in the army will probably never be equaled by another infantryman.

After the war, Murphy knew he did not want to go back to the life he had left behind in Texas. He did return to Texas briefly in 1945, but then he was featured on the cover of *Life Magazine* and his world changed dramatically. Actor James Cagney saw the cover and thought the youthful-faced young man could be a Hollywood star.

At first, Murphy had a hard time in Hollywood, even though Cagney was his teacher. But he eventually made forty-four films. The 1955 movie *To Hell and Back* was based on his autobiography, which was published under the same title.

Murphy was a contract actor. He signed long-term contracts with Universal Studios. The contract system disappeared in the 1960s, and Universal did not renew Murphy's contract. Gradually, work opportunities and movie assignments in Hollywood began to disappear, and he began to look for other business opportunities. Always a gambler, Murphy made and lost fortunes in his lifetime. He began to try desperate business deals and may even have become involved with mobsters or gangsters.

Murphy's life after the war was also haunted by the ghosts of his wartime memories. He suffered from what today is called post-traumatic stress syndrome. The symptoms are nervousness, sleeplessness, hallucinations, and inability to adjust to life in modern society.

Also during the 1930s, the Great Plains region suffered from a terrible drought, often referred to as the "Dust Bowl." Farmers' crops failed because there was no rain and severe dust storms blew across the prairies.

On May 28, 1971, Audie and several other men were passengers on a private plane. They were going to investigate a business opportunity. The plane crashed in fog and rain on the side of a mountain near Roanoke, Virginia. All aboard were killed. Audie Murphy was buried with full military honors at Arlington National Cemetery.

Chapter 1

CHILDHOOD

✳✳✳✳✳

Leon Audie Murphy was born June 20, 1924, near the small town of Kingston, Texas, in Hunt County, northeast of Dallas. Hunt County was cotton country in those days, and cotton was not an easy crop to produce. If there was a good season with plenty of cotton, prices were low. If there was a poor crop, prices were high. Either way, no one made much money, especially the sharecropper.

As a sharecropper, Emmett "Pat" Murphy did not own the land he lived on or the house that his family lived in. The house had a barn and an outhouse behind it. The home did not have plumbing or electricity. The family ate a lot of cornbread, gravy, and molasses. One wonders if Audie's slight build didn't come from a lack of good food

A filling station is another name for a gas station. Filling stations offered to top-off their customers' gas tanks, check the car's oil level, wash off the car's windshields, and dust out the floor mats—all at no extra charge. There are very few gas stations that would do all those things for free today.

as a growing child. Occasionally pork was on the table; more often, if there was meat, it was squirrel, rabbit, or dove. The whole family worked in the cotton fields. They planted, hoed weeds, and picked the crop. Audie went to work picking cotton by the time he was five.

✳✳✳

A Large Family

Audie was the sixth child born to his parents. There would eventually be twelve, though three died as children. The Murphy family was thought to be lazy. They had no education and seemed unable to improve themselves. Murphy's father was a friendly man who loved his children but did not support them. He also loved a bottle of whiskey and a good game of dominoes. Murphy's mother has been described as a sad, silent

woman who was frequently sick. When the next baby came along, she necessarily turned all her attention to that child. When Audie was replaced as the youngest, his oldest sister, Corinne, took responsibility for him. He saw her as a mother figure the rest of his life.

Audie was determined not to live like his family. As an older child, he read everything he could find in the library and drugstore book racks. There were no books in his home. He did well in school, as long as he could attend. None of his brothers or sisters seemed to have his ambition. Audie's father left home in 1940. The young boy dropped out of school and picked cotton to help support his family. He also worked in a grocery store and filling station in Greenville, Texas.

The family lived on one farm after another in the area. Sometimes they lived in a railroad boxcar. That kind of housing was for the poorest of the poor. Audie attended elementary school in the nearby small town of Celeste. He also lived near Farmersville and later in Greenville, Texas. The towns were all close together.

***

LEARNING TO SHOOT

As a young boy, Audie learned to hunt and shoot to put food on the family table. He was a good shot. He knew how to wait for the sound in the woods that meant a rabbit or squirrel had shown its hiding place. Audie's mother, Josie, died in 1941. She had several illnesses, but she really died from poverty and heartbreak. Audie felt guilty that he couldn't help her, and he regretted that all his adult life. He borrowed the money for her funeral and began to repay it when he joined the army. The funeral home forgave most of the debt.

After Audie became a hero, each town close to the area where Audie grew up claimed him as its favorite son and put on its own celebration in Audie's honor.

World War II saved Audie Murphy from his family's life. In 1938, German dictator Adolf Hitler began his march across Europe. He conquered every country in his path except Britain. He was joined by dictator Benito Mussolini of Italy. Japan joined Germany and Italy opposing the Allied Nations of the United States, Great Britain, France, and Russia. The United States was not directly involved in the war until the Japanese attack on Pearl Harbor, Hawaii on December 7, 1941. That event propelled America into the war on the side of the Allies.

Audie tried to enlist for military service, but he was rejected because he was too young (he was not yet eighteen). A few days after his eighteenth birthday, he signed the papers and enlisted in the infantry. He had been turned down by the Navy, Marines, and Army Paratroopers because he was too short. Most young men wanted to fly or be technical specialists. The infantry was for those, like Audie, who had no skills. He was sent to Camp Wolters, Texas, west of Fort Worth. It was the farthest he had ever been from home. His company commanders did not think him strong enough for battle. They tried to have Audie sent to bakers' and cooks' school, but Audie wanted to fight. Some soldiers nicknamed him "Baby," which he hated.

In training, he loved shooting, bayonet training, and camouflage work. Fellow soldiers remember that he could see little things in the landscape that others could not. Audie wrote home frequently from Camp Wolters, and his spelling and handwriting are like those of a young child.

He was sent to Fort Meade, Maryland, for advanced infantry training. Once again he had to fight to remain in the infantry. The army wanted to make him a clerk in the Post Exchange. Finally he was attached to Company B, First Battalion, Fifteenth Regiment,

U.S. Third Infantry Division. While at Fort Meade, he visited New York, Baltimore and Washington, D.C. Those trips gave him his first taste of big-city life.

Chapter 2

The War

✳✳✳✳✳

The Third Division went first to North Africa. Audie saw no action there. He was a messenger behind the lines and resented being assigned to a safe position. Then his company landed in southern Sicily in July 1943. At first he was again a runner, carrying messages back and forth behind the lines. He kept volunteering for patrols and finally saw front-line duty, close-range combat filled with danger, fatigue, and nervous strain. It was typical infantry warfare. Sometimes soldiers were close enough for eye contact with the enemy. If you could look someone in the eye, he became human and it was harder to kill him.

During World War II, the "Allies" was the name given to countries that joined with Great Britain to defeat Germany and Japan. The major Allied countries were United States, Great Britain, and Russia.

Summer and rainy weather made conditions bad for the soldiers. Audie soon was known for fighting hard to take and hold ground. He also gained a reputation as an effective warrior.

He killed his first men in Sicily. They were Italian officers, flushed from their hiding spot. Instead of surrendering, the two mounted magnificent white horses and began to ride away. Audie dropped to one knee and shot both of them. When someone later asked him why he had done it, he said, "It was my job, wasn't it?" Some have suggested that Audie saw killing the enemy much as he did hunting small game back in Texas. It was his job.

The company landed at Anzio, an Italian resort town, on January 22, 1944. An easy landing was followed by a strong German defense and some of the most bitter fight-

ing of the war. The combat took place in the mountains, which made it even more difficult. The company fought its way through to Rome, where they stayed several weeks. Audie was bored and homesick in Rome. While in Rome, he missed the Normandy invasion of June 6, perhaps the greatest action of World War II.

✳✳✳

AUDIE BECOMES A HERO

Finally, the Third Division moved on to southern France, where Audie once again strengthened his reputation. He wanted to see his comrades go home to their families and everyday lives. Audie had a survival instinct. Unfortunately, his good friend Lattie Tipton did not have that instinct. The two were cleaning out German sniper nests when from one nest a white flag was waved. Lattie said, "They want to surrender. I'm going to get them." Tipton went forward. "Don't trust them," Audie shouted. Tipton was killed as he stood up, and

Audie went crazy. He grabbed a German machine gun and raked the hill with bullets, time and time again. For his actions, Audie received the Distinguished Service Cross, the second-highest U.S. Army medal for valor, but he never forgot Tipton's death.

The Germans had fortified a quarry in southern France. They thought they could attack the Allied troops from the quarry without danger to themselves. Audie tossed a half case of grenades into the entrance to the fortification, and the attack stopped. Firing from the quarry also stopped. Later, two officers wanted a closer look. They took only four men with them. Audie sensed that something was wrong and stalked along behind them. He later said, "I figured those gentlemen were going to run into trouble, so I tagged along." Audie still had the hunt-

The French beaches of Normandy lie along the English Channel. On June 6, 1944, an Allied invasion began there and marked the great turning point of World War II in Europe. It was a difficult invasion, and many Allied soldiers died on those beaches.

ing instinct from his Texas days. The Germans attacked the detail and killed three men. The officers and one soldier dived into a shallow hole.

Behind them Audie called the name of every man in the patrol and waited for an answer. Once he knew the men's positions, he began to fire at the Germans. The Americans took the outpost and found a machine gun, four dead Germans, and three who were wounded. Audie was awarded the Silver Star.

Audie was often recommended for promotion to lieutenant, but he declined. He was embarrassed by his lack of education, and he didn't want to leave the men he had fought with for so long. In October 1944, he was promoted to 2nd Lieutenant in spite of himself. He insisted on two conditions: he would not have to help with the paperwork, and he would remain with Company B, Fifteenth Regiment, Third Division. As a 2nd Lieutenant Audie was responsible for the lives of thirty to forty men. His new position did not lessen the danger to himself. Instead, it increased as the enemy was eager to kill Allied officers. American officers wore stripes on the back of their helmets, both to let their men know who they were following, and to avoid recognition by the enemy from the front. Audie was often in the front lines, frequently leading soldiers into battle himself.

***

An Inglorious Wound

In house-to-house fighting in a small French town, Audie was shot in the right buttock. The sniper next fired at Audie's very visible helmet—only his head wasn't in the helmet. He had raised the helmet as a decoy. Meantime he fired his carbine at the Germans. Rain and mud

World War II was fought in two major parts of the world— the European theater and the Pacific theater. Audie Murphy never saw service in the Pacific.

made roads impassable. Audie had to wait three days to be taken to a hospital for treatment of his wound. He spent two months in a hospital in the city of Aix-en-Provence. Doctors treated the gangrene that had infected his wound. They had to remove large portions of one side of his buttocks to completely eliminate the dangerous infection.

Audie was back with Company B when a new German offensive began in January 1945. The Germans wanted to break through the American line at what they thought was its weakest point. This offensive led to Audie's greatest moment of heroism. It happened on January 26. Audie led his company to the edge of a forest. They dug foxholes in the frozen ground as best they could. Orders were to hold the position. They had little support, except two tank destroyers. The Germans outnumbered them and began to organize an attack. The Germans put the American tank destroyers out of action. Audie ordered his men to retreat into the forest. He planned to stay in place until the last minute.

Then he looked at one of the tank destroyers. Although it was burning, it still had a machine gun and ammunition. He climbed onto the destroyer and began firing the machine gun. While he fired he talked to headquarters on the radio. They asked how close the enemy was and he said, "Just hold the phone, and I'll let you talk to one. . . ." There were flames at his feet, which he claimed were warm for the first time during the war. Smoke surrounded him. When wind blew the smoke away, he saw that he had killed almost fifty Germans. The German infantry and their tanks withdrew. Audie was wounded slightly in the leg. As he walked away from the tank destroyer, it exploded. It could have exploded at any time he was in it. Audie's luck was with him. Reports vary, but the action lasted from thirty to sixty minutes. Audie received the Congressional Medal of Honor, the highest award given for bravery in action.

✳✳✳

WARTIME STORIES

Throughout his life Audie told wartime stories to friends and acquaintances. He recorded some stories in his autobiography *To Hell and Back*. One was about the time he broke the rules to rejoin Company B. He had been assigned to duty behind the lines. The army did not want the winner of a Congressional Medal of Honor killed. But Audie heard that Company B was in trouble. He grabbed a jeep and went to join his men. Murphy scolded them for giving up and eventually helped them out of the dangerous situation.

One story he didn't put in the book was about the time he went behind German lines and snuck up on a patrol unit. He could have killed them all with a hand grenade, but he turned away. They looked, he said later, just like American soldiers did. That kind of softening was not typical of Murphy.

By spring 1945, defeat of the Germans was clearly near. Ten thousand Germans had been taken prisoner. During the first week in May, those Germans remaining in the field surrendered. May 8 was declared V-E Day (Victory in Europe). Audie went to the French Riviera for "R and R," the common term for rest and recreation.

In mid-March, he was back in command of Company B, stationed in a small town near Salzburg, Germany. He officially received his Congressional Medal of Honor on June 2 at an airfield in Salzburg. He also received the French Legion of Merit, given for outstanding service. Audie was not yet twenty-one.

Chapter 3

A Hero Returns Home

✳✳✳✳✳

Audie Murphy was given the choice between remaining with the troops or going home to Texas. He chose to return to Texas so that he could, he thought, avoid being a hero in the spotlight. But when he landed in San Antonio on June 13, 1945, he was given a hero's welcome. Murphy tried to avoid the celebrations. He was shy when asked about his battle record. Reporters loved him all the more for his shyness. They followed him everywhere.

He went to the home of his sister, Corinne, in Farmersville. She and other family members claimed he had not changed at all. Although he had little connection to Farmersville, the town claimed him as one of their own and held a celebration the sec-

Life Magazine *featured classic photography and essays. From its founding in 1936 through the 1960s it was the most popular weekly magazine in America. To be on the cover of* Life *meant an individual was of great national importance.*

ond day he was home. Five thousand people filled the town square to hear speeches, a concert, and the reading of his citations. Audie was presented with war bonds. He spoke briefly. Then Greenville had a "Lt. Murphy Day." He spoke at a Rotary luncheon. Military and high school bands paraded. At a city hall ceremony, he was given $1,000. The town of McKinney held a celebration for Audie at its rodeo, and the VFW (Veterans of Foreign Wars) inducted him into membership.

Audie stayed in Farmersville with Corinne and her family. He visited wounded GIs in the hospital in McKinney, visited relatives, celebrated his twenty-first birthday in Dallas, and enjoyed the adoration of teenage girls.

James Cagney (1899-1986) was one of the most important movie stars of the 1940s and 1950s. His career lasted well into the 1980s. Like Murphy, he was a fairly short man—only 5'7".

✳✳✳

AUDIE IS A HERO AT HOME

Audie's big break came when he was featured on the cover of *Life Magazine* on July 16, 1945. The picture is a close-up portrait that shows his youthful face, his freckles, and his pleasant smile. He was in uniform and looked like an all-American hero. A photo essay inside featured several more pictures of him in Farmersville. The idea seemed to be that a small-town boy had made good and become a hero.

Audie's pleasant smile and manner hid the fact that he was constantly nervous and upset. Images of the war kept running through his mind. He had trouble sleeping and had bad nightmares. Sometimes he turned on all the lights to keep himself awake and avoid the nightmares. His family began to see that he wasn't unchanged. A sudden noise would startle him into defense, as though he were still in battle. Ordinary objects—once a bowl of black-eyed peas—suddenly brought images of war to his mind. Today these episodes are called flashbacks.

Talent scouts began to call on him after his face appeared on the cover of *Life*. Audie's first attempt at acting was a failure. Interstate Theaters, a motion picture chain, sponsored a weekly radio program called "Showtime" to promote its theaters. One segment of the program featured Audie. He was so shy that professional actors had to read his lines.

First-person accounts of his war experiences began to appear in newspapers across the country. They were called "A Hero Tells His Story" and were signed "A.L. Murphy." But they were written by a newspaper friend.

Audie's medals: Medal of Honor, Distinguished Service Cross, Silver Star with Oak Leaf Cluster, Legion of Merit, Bronze Star Medal with Oak Leaf Cluster, Purple Heart with two Oak Leaf Clusters, Croix de Guerre (two from France and one from Belguim), and the Combat Infantryman's Badge. An Oak Leaf Cluster signifies a subsequent award of the same decoration.

✳✳✳

AN ACTING CAREER BEGINS

After so much public attention, the people at Interstate Theaters

thought Audie might become an actor after all. Someone there knew

the actor James Cagney, who had a production company. Cagney

invited Audie to Hollywood. Audie had no real reason to stay in

Texas, and so he decided to move to Hollywood.

Chapter 4

HOLLYWOOD

✳✳✳✳✳

Audie once said he went to Hollywood because he liked the idea of making money. But it was several years before he made money. He arrived in Hollywood exhausted. He had spent almost three years at war and a summer appearing at festivals, celebrations and receptions. Cagney let him stay in a guest house at his home, and Audie lived there for several weeks. He had small-time acting offers but turned them all down. He wanted to be a good actor and agreed to take acting lessons. James Cagney and his brother found roles for him in their own productions or other film projects.

Audie had handicaps to overcome if he was to be a good actor. He walked like a farmer and had to be taught to walk all over again. He also had a heavy Texas drawl. It was good for character parts but not for most standard speech. Some listeners felt that Audie always retained a hint of Texas in his speech, and perhaps he did. Lifetime habits are hard to overcome.

He also took lessons in voice, acting, singing, and fencing.

Audie went to screen tests, but he did not get parts. James Cagney's studio had no parts for him. Audie moved out of the Cagney guest house. He slept in a gym operated by a friend. He lived on his army pension, which wasn't much.

He was also dating young actresses. Some found him too shy; others thought he was "country." Wanda Hendrix, who would become his first wife, liked him fine. Reporters also liked their romance. *Life Magazine* did a story on the couple. Wanda's agent got Audie a small part in a movie titled *Beyond Glory*.

To Hell and Back *was Universal Studio's highest earning picture from 1955 until 1975, when* Jaws *beat its record.*

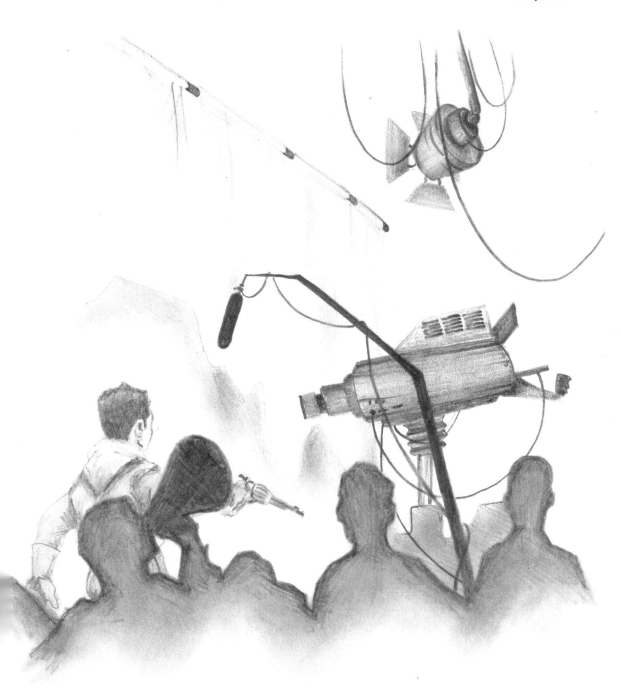

He also met David "Spec" McClure, the reporter who would help him write his autobiography. Spec got him a part in a bad movie titled *Texas, Brooklyn, and Heaven*. Audie decided that even though he was broke, he would be fussy about the roles he accepted.

Audie wrote two songs that made big hits, "Shutters and Boards" and "When the Wind Blows in Chicago."

✳✳✳

MARRIAGE AND A BOOK

The year 1948 was a big one for Audie. He married Wanda in January. His autobiography, *To Hell and Back*, was published in February. It got good reviews and made the *New York Times* bestseller list. Best of all, the book drew Hollywood's attention to Audie. He was given the starring role in the movie *Bad Boy*. The movie was about juvenile delinquency.

Universal Studios was one of the big, established movie studios in Hollywood. Because of the way Audie performed in *Bad Boy*, they signed him to a contract. They thought he would make a good cow-boy hero. His first Universal Studios picture was *The Kid from Texas*. He played a young, bad-guy cowboy. Audie was the misunderstood young outlaw in that movie and in others such as *The Cimarron Kid*. Then Wanda and Audie starred together in *Sierra*. The movie is not necessarily to blame, but their marriage ended. They divorced in 1951. Soon after, Audie married a flight attendant named Pam. They had two sons, and Audie seemed to settle down to being a family man.

One of his most important movie roles was in *The Red Badge of Courage*. The movie was based on Stephen Crane's classic novel about a young soldier in the Civil War. Audie had the opportunity to work with John Huston, a famous movie director. But studio editing of the movie

For his contribution to the motion picture industry, Audie Murphy has a star on the Hollywood Walk of Fame at 1601 Vine Street.

turned it into something that neither Huston nor Audie were proud of. Some think the best western he ever made was *No Name on the Bullet*. That became the title of one of the best biographies of Audie Murphy.

Audie's most successful movie was the screen version of his autobiography, *To Hell and Back*. He played himself, of course, and it was a difficult movie for him to make because it required that he relive his war experiences. Audie did not feel comfortable using his war record to promote his acting career and even suggested that someone else play himself in the movie.

✳✳✳

A CHANGING CAREER

Audie had many successes but also many failures. He was never able to develop films on his own. In the late

1950s Universal Studios reorganized. They were not successfully competing with westerns on TV. Audie began to appear in a few TV programs. There was a General Electric Theater Civil War drama, "Incident." He refused to do a series entitled "Medal of Honor" because it would play on his war record. He did play in "Whispering Smith," a series about a detective in Denver in the 1870s. But the series was not a critical success and was cancelled.

By the 1960s, movie studios had to compete even more with television westerns. Many American families had television sets in their living rooms. They could stay home and see a western. Why go to the movie theater? Universal thought Audie would draw them to the theaters. Between 1960-1965 he acted in several westerns, but all the movies had similar plots. One movie was not very different from the next.

In the early 1960s Audie started to take his career in a new direction. He began to write lyrics for country music. He had

The Six Day War was fought in 1967 between Israel and the Arab nations of Egypt, Syria, and Jordan. Israel expanded its territory as a result of victory in the war.

always liked country/western music, and now he found he had a talent for it. His songs were recorded by some of the best known singers of the day—Eddie Fisher, Charley Pride, Teresa Brewer, and Dean Martin.

In 1965, Audie's contract with Universal Studios was not renewed. At the age of forty-one, he was considered old for an actor. Other major western actors had retired, among them Gene Autry and Roy Rogers. 1968 was the first year since the late 1940s when Audie did not make a movie. In 1969, he starred in *A Time for Dying*.

✳✳✳

POST-TRAUMATIC STRESS

Throughout his Hollywood career, Audie was troubled by "battle fatigue." He still had nightmares and was nervous. He was often unable to sleep. His temper would flare unexpectedly. For a period, he was addicted to prescription drugs. (He beat the addiction by locking himself in a Florida hotel room and going through withdrawal without help or support.) He wasted money gambling. Wanda Hendrix later said that his nightmares and his attachment to his guns contributed to the end of their marriage. His marriage to Pam was also uncertain. He would leave and return, leave and return.

Today we call his condition "post-traumatic stress syndrome." The World War II name for it was "battle fatigue." Men were expected to readjust to civilian life, but some had a hard time leaving the war behind. Audie was one of them. He was one of the first to speak publicly about his troubles with battle fatigue and to suggest that more attention be paid to the mental health of returning soldiers.

Audie was rumored to be involved in a scheme to free labor union king Jimmy Hoffa from prison, though the claim was never substantiated. Jimmy Hoffa was suspected of having Mafia connections.

As his acting career went downhill, his need for money to pay debts and back taxes increased. He had bought an oil field several years before in the Middle East, but it was blown up during the Six Day War. This forced Murphy to declare bankruptcy, and he lost his ranches in Texas, Arizona and California, his plane, and other belongings. He became involved in shady deals, and was suspected of having connections with the Mafia.

✳✳✳

A FATAL BUSINESS TRIP

Audie Murphy was flying on a business trip on May 28, 1971, when the plane crashed into a mountain in West Virginia. All aboard were killed.

Audie Murphy was buried with full military honors at Arlington National Cemetery in Washington, D.C. At his request, the gravesite was marked with a plain tombstone, like that of a common soldier, with only his name, state, rank, and military decorations. In 1974, a large granite memorial was put up at the site of the airplane crash.

Many honors continue to be given to Murphy after his death. A veterans' hospital in San Antonio, Texas, was dedicated in his honor. The Texas State Legislature named June 20 as Audie Murphy Day in Texas. The Audie Murphy/American Cotton Museum in Greenville, Texas, holds the largest collection of personal items and memorabilia related to Murphy's life. The Audie Murphy Club was formed at Fort Hood, Texas. Non-commissioned officers in the army are elected to membership if their army records deserve special recognition. Although many are nominated, very few are chosen by the selection board. Members

Audie Murphy's gravesite is the second most visited site in Arlington National Cemetery. The first is the grave of President John F. Kennedy.

must show leadership in their concern for soldiers under their command and for their families.

In 2000, a United States postal stamp was dedicated in his honor.

Audie Murphy's life was marked first by hardship and tragedy and then by fame. Though his circumstances made him a household name, in the end he chose to remain anonymous.

Appendix A

EXCERPT FROM *To Hell and Back*

Audie Murphy's memoir of the war begins in Sicily. It has only a few references to his young life in Texas. The book is in present tense, which gives the reader a sense of what's happening. It is often a detailed description of war, violence, and death. Below is an excerpt:

It is the third day. The yellow, sputtering flame of the candle sends shadows skipping over the bearded faces of the men. In the flickering light, their strained, red eyes gleam like the eyes of caged animals.

The last of our water disappeared last night. Now thirst begins to torture our bodies. Lips crack; brains grow dizzy; talk becomes an effort.

We still have rations, but we dare not eat lest the food increase our thirst. Nerves stand on edge. We growl at one another and quarrel over trifles. Johnson's face is longer than usual; Kerrigan has lost his bubble; Snuffy cannot sleep; and Novak is out of coffee.

The book ends on an optimistic note:

I will go back. I will find the kind of girl of whom I once dreamed. I will learn to look at life through uncynical eyes, to have faith, to know love. I will learn to work in peace as in war. And finally—finally, like countless others, I will learn to live again.

Appendix B

MEDAL OF HONOR CITATION

The official U.S. Army citation for Audie Murphy's Medal of Honor reads:

Rank and organization: Second Lieutenant, U.S. Army, Company B 15th Infantry, 3rd Infantry Division.

Place and date: Near Holtzwihr France, 26 January, 1945.

Entered service at: Dallas, Texas. Birth: Hunt County, near Kingston, Texas.

G.O. No. 65, 9 August 1945.

Citation: Second Lt. Murphy commanded Company B, which was attacked by six tanks and waves of infantry. Lt. Murphy ordered his men to withdraw to prepared positions in a woods, while he remained forward at his command post and continued to give fire directions to the artillery by telephone. Behind him, to his right, one of our tank destroyers received a direct hit and began to burn. Its crew withdrew to the woods. Lt. Murphy continued to direct artillery fire, which killed large numbers of the advancing enemy infantry. With the enemy tanks abreast of his position, Lt. Murphy climbed on the burning tank destroyer, which was in danger of blowing up at any moment, and employed its .50 caliber machine gun against the enemy. He was alone and exposed to German fire from three sides, but his deadly fire killed dozens of Germans and caused their infantry attack to waver. The enemy tanks, losing infantry support, began to fall back. For an hour the Germans tried every available weapon to eliminate Lt. Murphy, but he continued to hold his position and wiped out a squad which was trying to creep up unnoticed on his right flank. Germans reached as close as 10 yards, only to be mowed down by his fire. He received a leg wound, but ignored it and continued his single-handed fight until his ammunition was exhausted. He then made his way back to his company, refused medical attention, and organized the company in a counterattack which forced the Germans to withdraw. His directing of artillery fire wiped out many of the enemy; he killed or wounded about 50. Lt. Murphy's indomitable courage and his refusal to give an inch of ground saved his company from possible encirclement and destruction, and enabled it to hold the woods which had been the enemy's objective.

Audie Murphy: War Hero and Movie Star

FILMOGRAPHY

Beyond Glory (1948)
Texas, Heaven and Brooklyn (1948)
Bad Boy (1949)
The Kid from Texas (1950)
Sierra (1950)
Kansas Raiders (1950)
The Red Badge of Courage (1951)
The Cimarron Kid (1952)
The Duel at Silver Creek (1952)
Gunsmoke (1953)
Column South (1953)
Tumbleweed (1953)
Ride Clear of Diablo (1954)
Drums Across the River (1954)
Destry (1954)
To Hell and Back (1955)
World in My Corner (1956)
Walk the Proud Land (1956)
Joe Butterfly (1957)
The Guns of Fort Petticoat (1957)
Night Passage (1957)
The Quiet American (1958)
Ride a Crooked Trail (1958)
The Gun Runners (1958)

No Name on the Bullet (1959)
The Wild and the Innocent (1959)
Cast a Long Shadow (1959)
The Unforgiven (1960)
Hell Bent for Leather (1960)
Seven Ways from Sundown (1960)
Posse from Hell (1961)
Battle at Bloody Beach (1961)
Six Black Horses (1962)
Showdown (1963)
Gunfight at Comanche Creek (1963)
The Quick Gun (1964)
Bullet for a Badman (1964)
Apache Rifles (1964)
Arizona Raiders (1965)
Gunpoint (1966)
The Texican (1966)
Trunk to Cairo (1966)
40 Guns to Apache Pass (1967)
A Time for Dying (1969)

Timeline

1924—born June 20

1940—father deserts family

1941—mother dies, leaving family orphaned; younger sisters and brother placed in Boles Home, an orphanage

1942—joins the infantry

1943—sees first combat in Sicily

1944—Distinguished Service Cross, for avenging the death of a friend by destroying enemy gunmen position; 2 Silver Stars; misses the June 6 Normandy invasion

1945—Congressional Medal of Honor for action near Holtzwihr in eastern France; V-E (Victory in Europe) Day May 7th; discharged September 21; returns to Texas briefly, is featured on cover of *Life Magazine*; goes to Hollywood

1949—marries Wanda Hendrix; stars in *Bad Boy*; autobiography, *To Hell and Back*, is published

1950—signs contract with Universal Studio, for which he did twenty-six films in fifteen years; divorce from Wanda Hendrix

1951—marries Pamela Archer

1952—son Terry Michael is born

1954—son James Shannon is born

1955—*To Hell and Back* movie becomes a box-office best-seller

1965—contract with Universal Studios expires and is not renewed

Mid-1960s—Murphy openly discusses his difficulties with post-traumatic stress syndrome

1971—dies in plane crash May 28, age 46; buried in Arlington National Cemetery, with a plain marker at his request, June 7

1973—November 11, dedication of Audie L. Murphy Memorial Veterans Hospital in San Antonio

1986—Sgt. Audie Murphy Club started at Fort Hood, Texas

1996—June 20 proclaimed Audie Murphy Day in Texas by the Texas Legislature

2000—Commemorative postage stamp issued in his honor

GLOSSARY

Camouflage—disguising things or people to fool the enemy. Soldiers often wore uniforms that were patterned to look like trees and bushes.

Carbine—a lightweight rifle with a shortened barrel used during World War II by officers and artillerymen

Comrade—another term for a friend or companion; someone you spend a lot of time with

Decoy—a trap or a lure; Audie raised his helmet to fool the Germans into thinking he was standing up.

Drought—dry weather, lack of rain

Filmography—a listing of motion pictures by actor, director, genre, etc.

Gangrene—the death of flesh due to lack of blood circulation or severe infection, in this case caused by a bullet wound. Sometimes caused by diabetes.

Infantry—soldiers who fight on foot with rifles, bayonets, hand grenades, machine guns, and mortars; as opposed to airmen, seamen, or cavalry (soldiers in armored vehicles)

Mafia—a secret organization of people dealing in illegal drugs and guns and other criminal activities; most members were traditionally of Sicilian or Italian descent

Malnutrition—a diet that does not have the vitamins and minerals and materials needed to support growth and health

Memorabilia—items such as news clippings, letters, pictures, or other physical items relating to the life of the person remembered, not always a famous person; your relatives can have memorabilia

Quarry—an enormous hole in the ground, from which stone is dug; most quarries can hold several vehicles and many men

Sharecropper—a tenant farmer who pays a share of his crop to the landowner as rent

Sicily—an island south of Italy that is part of that country and separated from it by a narrow band of water known as the Straits of Messina

Tank Destroyer—a lightly-armored vehicle mounted with a large cannon capable of penetrating tank armor

Warrior—another term for a soldier, or one who fights in battle

AUTHOR'S NOTE

There are few full books that deal with Audie Murphy's life. One is his autobiography, *To Hell and Back*, which I have read but don't recommend for young readers because it details his wartime experiences. Don Graham's *No Name on the Bullet* (New York: Viking, 1989) is a scholarly, thoughtful, and thoroughly researched piece of work. I have relied on it a great deal, and I am indebted to Don for unraveling the mystery of America's most decorated war hero. Young readers should be indebted to him too.

WEBSITES

http://www.mdw.army.mil/content/anmviewer.asp?a-140

http://www.jrotc.org/audie_murphy.htm

http://en.wikipedia.org/wiki/Audie_Murphy

http://www.tsha.utexas.edu/handbook/online/articles/MM/fmu13.html

www.audiemurphy.com
(Official website for the Audie Murphy Foundation)

INDEX

Praise for the Stars of Texas Series:

". . . an excellent series." –*The Manhattan Mercury*

"The best way to build up a new generation of Texas history lovers is to produce books that appeal to young readers, and the good folks at State House Press are opening that door with a wonderful new series . . . 'The Stars of Texas Series' is going to be something to watch. . . . The books are fast-paced and interesting, allowing the student to quickly understand the customs and life ways of Texas history." –*Texas Illustrated Magazine*

Praise for *Henrietta King: Rancher and Philanthropist*:

". . . the kids will love the book, not realizing that it is 'good for them.'" –*Round-up Magazine*

". . . a fine book . . . *Henrietta King* has opened the door to interest young readers to history." –*The Manhattan Mercury*

"If you want to expose your children to a truly remarkable woman, get this book." –*Eclectic Homeschool On-line*

Praise for *Mirabeau B. Lamar: Second President of Texas*:

"Alter lets us see Lamar against the background of his era. With style and clarity, this book enables youngsters to understand a fairly complex character and his contribution to Texas history. Highly recommended for juvenile readers." –*Review of Texas Books*

". . . the children will be so engrossed in this well-written book, . . . that the kids will never realize they are reading something 'good for them.' They will only know that they are reading a good story." –*Round-up Magazine*

"a much needed text for teaching the TEKS in Texas." –Leslie Woolsey, Region XI Educational Services Center

"*Mirabeau B. Lamar* is an excellent, youth-oriented introduction to one of early Texas' histories most important figures. This book, and others in the Stars of Texas series, offers not only excellent text, but a timeline, glossary, suggestions for further reading, websites, and an index." –*Eclectic Homeschool On-line*

Praise for *Miriam "Ma" Ferguson: First Woman Governor of Texas*:

"Recommended reading for grades 4-7: Good for research and clarity in presentation of ideas." –Carmen Antoine, Region XI Educational Service Center

"A highly valued addition to school library 'American History & Biography' collections, and 'Texas History' reading lists, *Miriam 'Ma' Ferguson* is very strongly recommended as an informative and inspiring introduction to the life and times of the Ferguson family." –*Midwest Book Review*

"her story makes for fascinating reading. Intended for ages 9-12, this 72-page, 7x9, hardcover book offers Miriam Ferguson's tale in a highly readable format that will interest children of all ages." –*Eclectic Homeschool On-line*

"a much needed text for teaching the TEKS in Texas"

Stars
of
Texas
Series

The series which focuses on important, but perhaps lesser known, Texans and their contributions to Texas history.

Audie Murphy
War Hero and Movie Star

Judy Alter
Illustrated by Patrick Messersmith

978-1-933337-12-8
$14.95
May 2008

Ann Richards
"A Woman's Place is in the Dome"

April D. Stumpff
Illustrated by Patrick Messersmith

978-1-933337-19-7
$14.95

Henrietta King
Rancher and Philanthropist

Judy Alter
Illustrated by Carryle Messersmith

Mirabeau B. Lamar
Second President of Texas

Judy Alter
Illustrated by Patrick Messersmith

Miriam "Ma" Ferguson
First Woman Governor of Texas

Judy Alter
Illustrated by Patrick Messersmith

Martín de León
Tejano Empresario

Judy Alter
Illustrated by Patrick Messersmith

978-1-880510-98-8
$17.95

978-1-880510-97-1
$17.95

978-1-933337-01-2
$17.95

978-1-933337-08-1
$14.95

State ★ House
Press

Revealing the past one page at a time

**Use code 3B
to receive a 30% discount when ordering!**

Distributed by
Texas A&M University Press Consortium
1-800-826-8911 ★ www.tamu.edu/upress